Principles of Accounting

SECOND EDITION

Working Papers IIA / Chapters 15–28

Belverd E. Needles, Jr.
DePaul University
Chicago

Henry R. Anderson
University of
Central Florida

James C. Caldwell
Arthur Andersen & Co.
Dallas/Fort Worth

Houghton Mifflin Company   Boston
Dallas   Geneva, Illinois   Hopewell, New Jersey   Palo Alto

Printed in the U.S.A.

Library of Congress Catalog Card Number: 83-80989

ISBN: 0-395-34335-6

CDEFGHIJ-A-898765

To the Student

This book contains working papers to be used in preparing solutions to all A problems in Chapters 15 through 28. The working papers are designed to simplify your work: appropriate forms for each problem are provided, and some preliminary information has been printed to help you get started.

This book also presents, at the beginning, a special work sheet analysis and financial statements for companies using the periodic inventory method. Reading this analysis will help you do the problems in Chapter 22. A similar work sheet analysis and financial statements, dealing with companies that use the perpetual inventory method, are provided for Chapter 23.

Work Sheet Analyses for Chapters 22 and 23

Chapter 22 Work Sheet Analysis

WORK SHEET AND FINANCIAL STATEMENTS FOR COMPANIES USING PERIODIC INVENTORIES

The year-end work sheet for a manufacturing company using a periodic inventory approach is very much like that for a merchandiser. The only real difference is that the work sheet for a manufacturer has two extra columns for the statement of cost of goods manufactured. In this appendix to Chapter 22, we will continue our analysis of the Pedersen Company. Data from the company's records have already been used in the chapter to illustrate cost flow and the calculation of cost of goods manufactured. Pedersen Company's work sheet for the year ending December 31, 19xx, is shown in Figure 22A-1 (next two pages). Below is a full explanation of the year-end accounting procedures. Income statement account balances are the same as those used in Figures 22-9 and 22-10.

The Trial Balance Columns

Work sheet analysis begins with the taking of a trial balance. The first two columns in Figure 22A-1 represent the trial balance. As its name implies, a trial balance lists all general ledger accounts and their balances to prove that the unadjusted accounts are in balance.

Year-End Adjusting Entries

Account balances in the general ledger at year end are the cumulative effect of all transactions recorded during the year. However, some accounts change simply from the passage of time rather than from a transaction. Year-end adjusting entries are prepared so that this type of information can be entered into the accounting records. General journal entries and explanations for the Adjustments columns in Figure 22A-1 follow.

(a) Depreciation Expense, Machinery and Equipment	14,800	
Accumulated Depreciation, Machinery and Equipment		14,800
To record depreciation of machinery for the period		
(b) Depreciation Expense, Factory Building	16,200	
Accumulated Depreciation, Factory Building		16,200
To record depreciation of factory building for the period		
(c) Small Tools Expense	2,700	
Small Tools		2,700
To write off small tools used		

Figure 22A-1
Work Sheet
Analysis—
Manufacturing
Company—
Periodic
Inventories

Pedersen Company
Work Sheet
For the Year Ended December 31, 19xx

Account Titles	Trial Balance Debit	Trial Balance Credit	Adjustments Debit	Adjustments Credit	Adjusted Trial Balance Debit	Adjusted Trial Balance Credit	Statement of Cost of Goods Manufactured Debit	Statement of Cost of Goods Manufactured Credit	Income Statement Debit	Income Statement Credit	Balance Sheet Debit	Balance Sheet Credit
Cash	24,600				24,600						24,600	
Accounts Receivable	65,000				65,000						65,000	
Allowance for Uncollectible Accounts		1,200				1,200						1,200
Materials Inventory	17,500				17,500		17,500	20,400			20,400	
Work in Process Inventory	21,200				21,200		21,200	23,500			23,500	
Finished Goods Inventory	70,000				70,000				70,000	76,500	76,500	
Prepaid Insurance	4,800			(d) 1,600	3,200						3,200	
Machinery and Equipment	138,500				138,500						138,500	
Accumulated Depreciation, Machinery and Equipment		49,700		(a) 14,800		64,500						64,500
Factory Building	294,800				294,800						294,800	
Accumulated Depreciation, Factory Building		108,000		(b) 16,200		124,200						124,200
Small Tools Expense	9,800			(c) 2,700	7,100						7,100	
Accounts Payable		26,100				26,100						26,100
Notes Payable—8½%, due in 5 years		100,000				100,000						100,000
Capital Stock—no par value		250,000				250,000						250,000
Retained Earnings, Beginning		50,000				50,000						50,000

2

Account	Trial Balance Dr	Trial Balance Cr	Adjustments Dr	Adjustments Cr	Adjusted Trial Balance Dr	Adjusted Trial Balance Cr	Cost of Goods Manufactured Dr	Cost of Goods Manufactured Cr	Income Statement Dr	Income Statement Cr	Balance Sheet Dr	Balance Sheet Cr
Sales		750,000				750,000				750,000		
Materials Purchases	142,600				142,600		142,600					
Direct Labor	199,000				199,000		199,000					
Indirect Labor	46,400				46,400		46,400					
Power	25,200				25,200		25,200					
Supervision	37,900				37,900		37,900					
Other Factory Costs	11,400				11,400		11,400					
Sales Salaries and Commissions Expense	46,500				46,500				46,500			
Advertising Expense	19,500				19,500				19,500			
Other Selling Expenses	7,400				7,400				7,400			
Administrative Salaries Expense	65,000				65,000				65,000			
Franchise and Property Taxes Expense	72,000				72,000				72,000			
Other General and Administrative Expenses	11,300				11,300				11,300			
Interest Expense	4,600				4,600				4,600			
	1,335,000	1,335,000										
Depreciation Expense, Machinery and Equipment			(a) 14,800		14,800		14,800					
Depreciation Expense, Factory Building			(b) 16,200		16,200		16,200					
Small Tools Expense			(c) 2,700		2,700		2,700					
Factory Insurance Expense			(d) 1,600		1,600		1,600					
Federal Income Tax Expense			(e) 11,548		11,548				11,548			
Federal Income Taxes Payable				(e) 11,548		11,548						11,548
			46,848	46,848	1,377,548	1,377,548		43,900				
Cost of Goods Manufactured to Income Statement								492,600	492,600			
							536,500	536,500	800,448	826,500	627,548	653,600
Net Income After Taxes to Balance Sheet									26,052			26,052
									826,500	826,500	653,600	653,600

(d) Factory Insurance Expense   1,600
        Prepaid Insurance   1,600
            To charge to expense that part of
            prepaid insurance premiums that
            expired during the period

(e) Federal Income Tax Expense   11,548
        Federal Income Taxes Payable   11,548
            To record federal income taxes for
            the period

Accounting for Inventories

The Pedersen Company used the periodic method of accounting for inventories. Physical counts are made at year end to find out the amount and stage of completion of goods on hand. After assigning costs to the year-end inventories, the Pedersen Company had the following ending balances: $20,400 in Materials Inventory, $23,500 in Work in Process Inventory, and $76,500 in Finished Goods Inventory.

As shown in Figure 22-10, the beginning and ending balances of Materials Inventory and Work in Process Inventory are used in computing cost of goods manufactured. For this reason, these amounts are entered in the debit column for the Statement of Cost of Goods Manufactured in the work sheet (Figure 22A-1). Beginning balances are carried as debits from the Adjusted Trial Balance columns to the debit column for Statement of Cost of Goods Manufactured. These amounts, in effect, are treated as additional expenses to those incurred during the period. Ending balances for Materials Inventory and Work in Process Inventory are credited, because they represent unused costs. They are subtracted from total manufacturing costs incurred to arrive at the cost of goods manufactured. These ending balances are also carried over to the Balance Sheet columns as assets (debits).

The same reasoning is used to explain the work sheet treatment of Finished Goods Inventory. Beginning and ending Finished Goods Inventory balances are used to compute cost of goods sold. For this reason, the beginning balance is carried to the Income Statement columns as a debit. The ending balance is credited to the Income Statement columns and debited to the Balance Sheet columns as an asset.

Statement of Cost of Goods Manufactured Columns

In addition to the beginning and ending balances of the Materials Inventory and Work in Process Inventory, all balances of expense accounts for the manufacturing process are carried from the Adjusted Trial Balance to the Statement of Cost of Goods Manufactured columns. The difference between total debits and total credits in these columns is the cost of goods manufactured for the year. In Figure 22A-1, the amount is $492,600. This amount is the same as in Figure 22-10. In our example, the statement of cost of goods manufactured was prepared prior to this discussion of the work sheet. Before proceeding, therefore, trace each item in these two columns to the actual statement in Figure 22-10. Doing so will help you to prepare this kind of statement.

Income Statement Columns

On the work sheet, the cost of goods manufactured is transferred to the income statement by crediting the Statement of Cost of Goods Manufactured and debiting the Income Statement columns. We must now determine the remaining amount to be carried over to the Income Statement columns. The credit amount for Sales must be extended from the Adjusted Trial Balance to the Income Statement columns. We have already discussed beginning and ending balances of Finished Goods Inventory. Other relevant account balances include Selling Expense accounts, General and Administrative Expense accounts, Interest Expense, and Federal Income Tax Expense. The income statement was also prepared and discussed before developing this work sheet. Generally, this sequence is reversed, and the income statement is prepared from data in these two columns of the work sheet. Trace all amounts from the work sheet columns to the actual income statement in Figure 22-9 to make sure you understand the relationship between these two documents.

Closing Entries

All account balances used in computing cost of goods manufactured and net income are closed to Retained Earnings at year end. Below are the closing entries for the Pedersen Company. Detailed explanations are also shown. The Manufacturing Summary account acts as the clearinghouse account for the cost of goods manufactured statement. In much the same way, the Income Summary account is related to the income statement in the closing procedures. When the periodic inventory method is used, ending inventory balances are also established when closing entries are prepared. Ending inventory balances are entered into the records when these entries are posted to the general ledger.

Dec. 31	Manufacturing Summary	536,500	
	Materials Inventory, Jan. 1, 19xx		17,500
	Work in Process Inventory, Jan. 1, 19xx		21,200
	Materials Purchases		142,600
	Direct Labor		199,000
	Indirect Labor		46,400
	Power		25,200
	Supervision		37,900
	Other Factory Costs		11,400
	Depreciation Expense, Machinery and Equipment		14,800
	Depreciation Expense, Factory Building		16,200
	Small Tools Expense		2,700
	Factory Insurance Expense		1,600
	To close manufacturing accounts and beginning Materials and Work in Process Inventory balances to Manufacturing Summary		

Dec. 31	Materials Inventory, Dec. 31, 19xx	20,400	
	Work in Process Inventory, Dec. 31, 19xx	23,500	
	Manufacturing Summary		43,900
	To establish year-end balances in		
	the Materials and Work in Process		
	Inventory accounts and to remove		
	these costs from the Manufacturing		
	Summary account		
31	Income Summary	800,448	
	Finished Goods Inventory, Jan 1, 19xx		70,000
	Sales Salaries and Commissions		
	Expense		46,500
	Advertising Expense		19,500
	Other Selling Expenses		7,400
	Administrative Salaries Expense		65,000
	Franchise and Property Taxes Expense		72,000
	Other General and Administrative		
	Expenses		11,300
	Interest Expense		4,600
	Federal Income Tax Expense		11,548
	Manufacturing Summary		492,600
	To close income statement expenses		
	and beginning Finished Goods		
	Inventory balance to Income		
	Summary		
31	Sales	750,000	
	Finished Goods Inventory, Dec. 31, 19xx	76,500	
	Income Summary		826,500
	To close Sales to Income Summary		
	account and to set up the ending		
	balance in Finished Goods Inventory		
31	Income Summary	26,052	
	Retained Earnings		26,052
	To close Income Summary account		
	and transfer balance to Retained		
	Earnings		

Balance Sheet Columns

The final two columns in the work sheet represent the year-end balance sheet. All asset, liability, and stockholders' equity account balances are carried from the Adjusted Trial Balance to the Balance Sheet columns. The year-end net income is also credited to the balance sheet. The resulting December 31, 19xx, balance sheet for the Pedersen Company is shown in Figure 22A-2. Trace all amounts in the Balance Sheet columns on the work sheet to the actual balance sheet to make sure it is accurate.

**Figure 22A-2
The Balance
Sheet**

**Pedersen Company
Balance Sheet
December 31, 19xx**

Assets

Current Assets		
Cash		$ 24,600
Accounts Receivable	$ 65,000	
Less Allowance for Uncollectible Accounts	1,200	63,800
Materials Inventory		20,400
Work in Process Inventory		23,500
Finished Goods Inventory		76,500
Prepaid Insurance		3,200
Small Tools Expense		7,100
Total Current Assets		$219,100
Plant and Equipment		
Machinery and Equipment	$138,500	
Less Accumulated Depreciation	64,500	$ 74,000
Factory Building	$294,800	
Less Accumulated Depreciation	124,200	170,600
Total Plant and Equipment		244,600
Total Assets		$463,700

Liabilities

Current Liabilities		
Accounts Payable	$ 26,100	
Income Taxes Payable	11,548	
Total Current Liabilities		$ 37,648
Long-Term Debt		
Notes Payable (8½% due in five years)		100,000
Total Liabilities		$137,648

Stockholders' Equity

Capital Stock		$250,000
Retained Earnings, January 1, 19xx	$ 50,000	
Net Income for 19xx	26,052	
Retained Earnings, December 31, 19xx		76,052
Total Stockholders' Equity		326,052
Total Liabilities and Stockholders' Equity		$463,700

WORK SHEET AND FINANCIAL STATEMENTS
FOR COMPANIES USING PERPETUAL INVENTORIES

The purpose of this appendix is to show how to prepare the work sheet and financial statements when a company uses the perpetual inventory method. Be sure to review this appendix before starting the practice set Aluma-Cylinder Company, Inc., by Henry R. Anderson and Carol A. Gordon.

Information from the Pedersen Company analysis in Chapter 22 is used in this analysis. However, the numbers and financial results are not identical. Compare this analysis with that in Chapter 22. You will see the differences in preparing work sheets and financial statements when a company uses a perpetual versus a periodic inventory approach.

We begin with the trial balance for the Pedersen Company. It was prepared after all the normal transactions for December 19xx were posted.

Next, subsidiary ledgers are reconciled with the inventory control accounts in the general ledger. They reveal the following information:

Materials Ledger:	Material AC	$10,100
	Material DG	8,900
	Operating Supplies	1,400
	Total	$20,400

Job Order Cost Cards:	Job 20-045	$20,100
	Job 20-046	3,400
	Total	$23,500

Finished Goods Ledger:	Product 20	$ 2,900
	Product 34	47,700
	Product 61	25,900
	Total	$76,500

The subsidiary ledger for overhead costs contains the following items. They support the unadjusted balance of Factory Overhead Control on December 31:

Indirect labor	$36,150
Operating supplies	27,600
Heat, light, and power	16,140
Repairs and maintenance	24,620
Plant supervision salaries	16,390
Total	$120,900

Year-end adjusting entries are needed for the following items:

a. Depreciation of machinery and equipment for the year was $14,800. Depreciation of the factory building was $16,200.
b. Small tools costing $2,700 were used during the year.
c. Prepaid insurance of $1,600 expired during 19xx.
d. Accrued payroll data at year end included direct labor wages, $1,450 (Job 20-046); indirect labor wages, $890; administrative salaries, $1,220; FICA taxes payable, $214; and federal income taxes payable, employees, $925.

Pedersen Company
Trial Balance
December 31, 19xx

	Debit	Credit
Cash	$ 24,600	
Accounts Receivable	65,000	
Allowance for Uncollectible Accounts		$ 1,200
Materials Inventory Control	20,400	
Work in Process Inventory Control	23,500	
Finished Goods Inventory Control	76,500	
Prepaid Insurance	4,800	
Machinery and Equipment	138,500	
Accumulated Depreciation, Machinery and Equipment		49,700
Factory Building	294,800	
Accumulated Depreciation, Factory Building		108,000
Small Tools Expense	9,800	
Accounts Payable		26,100
Wages and Salaries Payable		—
FICA Taxes Payable		—
Federal Income Taxes Payable, Employees		—
Notes Payable, 8½% due in 5 years		100,000
Capital Stock—$10 par value		250,000
Retained Earnings		21,800
Sales		750,000
Cost of Goods Sold	459,600	
Factory Payroll	—	
Factory Overhead Control	120,900	
Factory Overhead Applied		157,900
Sales Salaries and Commissions Expense	46,500	
Advertising Expense	19,500	
Other Selling Expenses	7,400	
Administrative Salaries	65,000	
Franchise and Property Taxes Expense	72,000	
Other General and Administrative Expenses	11,300	
Interest Expense	4,600	
	$1,464,700	$1,464,700

e. After adjustments **a** through **d** have been posted to the work sheet, the Overhead Control and Overhead Applied accounts should be closed and any difference debited or credited to Cost of Goods Sold.

f. Interest expense of $1,250 is payable at year end.

g. Federal income tax is 50 percent of pretax net income.

Adjusting Journal Entries

From the data just given, we prepare the following journal entries:

a. Factory Overhead Control   31,000
    Accumulated Depreciation, Machinery and
      Equipment   14,800
    Accumulated Depreciation, Factory
      Building   16,200
      To record depreciation of machinery and
      factory building for the period

b. Factory Overhead Control   2,700
    Small Tools Expense   2,700
      To write off small tools used during the
      period

c. Factory Overhead Control   1,600
    Prepaid Insurance   1,600
      To charge to expense that portion of
      prepaid insurance premiums that expired
      during the period

d. Work in Process Inventory Control (Job 20-046)   1,450
    Factory Overhead Control   890
    Administrative Salaries Expense   1,220
      FICA Taxes Payable   214
      Federal Income Taxes Payable, Employees   925
      Wages and Salaries Payable   2,421
      To record payroll liability for last six days
      of year and to distribute factory payroll
      to production accounts

e. Factory Overhead Applied   157,900
    Factory Overhead Control   157,090
    Cost of Goods Sold   810
      To close out factory overhead account
      balances and to dispose of overapplied
      amount

f. Interest Expense   1,250
    Interest Payable   1,250
      To record interest payable on note at year
      end

g. Federal Income Tax Expense	31,220	
Federal Income Taxes Payable, Company		31,220
To record federal taxes on company		
income for the period		

The Work Sheet

Pedersen Company's work sheet for 19xx is shown in Figure 23A-1 (next two pages). After the adjusting entries are posted, amounts can be extended to the columns for Adjusted Trial Balance, Income Statement, and Balance Sheet. Note that there are no columns for cost of goods manufactured. When perpetual inventories and a job order cost system are used, all manufacturing costs are assigned to the Work in Process Inventory, Finished Goods Inventory, or Cost of Goods Sold account in the general ledger. Most of the data needed to prepare the statement of cost of goods manufactured are taken from subsidiary ledgers. The actual cost of goods manufactured cannot be determined from accounts shown on the work sheet because it is part of the total cost of goods sold. Net income for the period, after taxes, is $31,220.

Accounting for Inventories

In the work sheet analysis in Chapter 22, the trial balance included beginning-of-year balances for the three inventory accounts. We followed a special accounting procedure to close out these balances and establish the year-end balances used to prepare the financial statements. In our present example, we are using perpetual inventories. Therefore, the general ledger balances in the three inventory control accounts are always current. There is no need to make special adjustments to these accounts on the work sheet. For purposes of preparing the statement of cost of goods manufactured, inventory balances on January 1, 19xx, were as follows: Materials Inventory Control, $17,500; Work in Process Inventory Control, $21,200; and Finished Goods Inventory Control, $70,000.

Statement of Cost of Goods Manufactured

Before we can prepare the statement of cost of goods manufactured, some supporting data are needed. Purchases of materials and supplies during 19xx totaled $145,075, and $142,175 of these items were issued to production. The issued items included $27,600 of operating supplies charged to Factory Overhead Control. Direct labor for the year, before year-end adjustments, totaled $197,375. When overhead is applied to production by using an overhead rate, the amount applied should be used in preparing the statement of cost of goods manufactured. This statement is shown in Figure 23A-2 (page 14).

The treatment of the $27,600 of supplies charged to factory overhead should be explained. Operating supplies are a part of Materials Inventory Control. If the $27,600 were ignored in computing the Cost of Materials Used, the amount would also include supplies used. However, this amount has already been charged to factory overhead and makes up a part of the factory overhead applied to production. Therefore, to avoid including the $27,600 twice, we must subtract it when computing the amount for Cost of Materials Used.

11

Figure 23A-1
Work Sheet Analysis—Manufacturing Company—Perpetual Inventories

Pedersen Company
Work Sheet
For the Year Ended December 31, 19xx

Account Names	Trial Balance Debit	Trial Balance Credit	Adjustments Debit	Adjustments Credit	Adjusted Trial Balance Debit	Adjusted Trial Balance Credit	Income Statement Debit	Income Statement Credit	Balance Sheet Debit	Balance Sheet Credit
Cash	24,600				24,600				24,600	
Accounts Receivable	65,000				65,000				65,000	
Allowance for Uncollectible Accounts		1,200				1,200				1,200
Materials Inventory Control	20,400				20,400				20,400	
Work in Process Inventory Control	23,500		(d) 1,450		24,950				24,950	
Finished Goods Inventory Control	76,500				76,500				76,500	
Prepaid Insurance	4,800			(c) 1,600	3,200				3,200	
Machinery and Equipment	138,500				138,500				138,500	
Accumulated Depreciation, Machinery and Equipment		49,700		(a) 14,800		64,500				64,500
Factory Building	294,800				294,800				294,800	
Accumulated Depreciation, Factory Building		108,000		(a) 16,200		124,200				124,200
Small Tools Expense	9,800			(b) 2,700	7,100				7,100	
Accounts Payable		26,100				26,100				26,100
Wages and Salaries Payable				(d) 2,421		2,421				2,421
FICA Taxes Payable				(d) 214		214				214
Federal Income Taxes Payable, Employees				(d) 925		925				925

12

Account	Trial Balance Dr	Trial Balance Cr	Adjustments Dr	Adjustments Cr	Adjusted Trial Balance Dr	Adjusted Trial Balance Cr	Income Statement Dr	Income Statement Cr	Balance Sheet Dr	Balance Sheet Cr
Notes Payable, 8½%, due in 5 years		100,000				100,000				100,000
Capital Stock—$10 par value		250,000				250,000				250,000
Retained Earnings		21,800				21,800				21,800
Sales		750,000				750,000		750,000		
Cost of Goods Sold	459,600			(e) 810	458,790		458,790			
Factory Payroll			(a) 31,000		—					
Factory Overhead Control	120,900		(b) 2,700 (c) 1,600 (d) 890	(e) 157,090	—					
Factory Overhead Applied		157,900	(e) 157,900			—				
Sales Salaries and Commissions Expense	46,500				46,500		46,500			
Advertising Expense	19,500				19,500		19,500			
Other Selling Expenses	7,400				7,400		7,400			
Administrative Salaries Expense	65,000		(d) 1,220		66,220		66,220			
Franchise and Property Taxes Expense	72,000				72,000		72,000			
Other General and Administrative Expenses	11,300				11,300		11,300			
Interest Expense	4,600		(f) 1,250		5,850		5,850			
Interest Payable				(f) 1,250		1,250				1,250
Federal Income Tax Expense			(g) 31,220		31,220		31,220			
Federal Income Tax Payable, Company				(g) 31,220		31,220				31,220
	1,464,700	1,464,700	229,230	229,230	1,373,830	1,373,830	718,780	750,000	623,830	
Net Income After Taxes to Balance Sheet							31,220			31,220
							750,000	750,000	655,050	655,050

Pedersen Company
Statement of Cost of Goods Manufactured
For the Year Ended December 31, 19xx

Materials Used		
Materials Inventory Control,		
January 1, 19xx	$ 17,500	
Materials and Supplies Purchased	145,075	
Cost of Materials Available for Use	$162,575	
Less: Materials Inventory Control,		
December 31, 19xx	(20,400)	
Supplies Charged to		
Factory Overhead	(27,600)	
Cost of Materials Used		$114,575
Direct Labor		197,375
Factory Overhead Applied		157,900
Total Manufacturing Costs		$469,850
Plus Work in Process Inventory Control,		
January 1, 19xx		21,200
Total Costs in Process During the Year		$491,050
Less Work in Process Inventory Control,		
December 31, 19xx		(24,950)
Cost of Goods Manufactured		$466,100

Income Statement and Balance Sheet

The income statement and balance sheet for the Pedersen Company for 19xx are illustrated in Figures 23A-3 and 23A-4 (next two pages).

Closing Entries

Closing entries are much simpler when perpetual inventories and a job order cost system are being used. The Factory Overhead Control and Factory Overhead Applied accounts have already been closed as part of the process of adjusting journal entries. The Factory Payroll account goes down to a zero balance each time payroll is distributed to the production accounts. Beginning inventory balances do not have to be canceled and ending balances established. Ending balances already exist. Therefore, the only general ledger accounts remaining that must be closed are Sales, Cost of Goods Sold, the operating expenses, Interest Expense, and Federal Income Tax Expense.

Dec. 31	Sales	750,000	
	Income Summary		750,000
	To close Sales to the Income Summary account		
31	Income Summary	718,780	
	Cost of Goods Sold		458,790
	Sales Salaries and Commissions Expense		46,500
	Advertising Expense		19,500
	Other Selling Expenses		7,400
	Administrative Salaries Expense		66,220
	Franchise and Property Taxes Expense		72,000
	Other General and Administrative Expenses		11,300
	Interest Expense		5,850
	Federal Income Tax Expense		31,220
	To close Cost of Goods Sold and expense accounts to Income Summary		
31	Income Summary	31,220	
	Retained Earnings		31,220
	To close Income Summary to Retained Earnings		

Pedersen Company
Income Statement
For the Year Ended December 31, 19xx

Net Sales		$750,000
Cost of Goods Sold		
Beginning Finished Goods Inventory Control	$ 70,000	
Cost of Goods Manufactured (see Figure 23A-2)	466,100	
Total Cost of Finished Goods Available for Sale	$536,100	
Less: Ending Finished Goods Inventory Control	(76,500)	
Overapplied Overhead	(810)	
Cost of Goods Sold		$458,790
Gross Profit on Sales		$291,210
Operating Expenses		
Selling Expenses		
Salaries and Commissions Expense	$46,500	
Advertising Expense	19,500	
Other Selling Expenses	7,400	
Total	$ 73,400	
General and Administrative Expenses		
Administrative Salaries Expense	$66,220	
Franchise and Property Taxes Expense	72,000	
Other General and Administrative Expenses	11,300	
Total	149,520	
Total Operating Expenses		222,920
Income from Operations		$ 68,290
Less Interest Expense		5,850
Income Before Income Taxes		$ 62,440
Federal Income Taxes		31,220
Net Income		$ 31,220

Figure 23A-4
Balance Sheet

Pedersen Company
Balance Sheet
December 31, 19xx

Assets

Current Assets			
Cash		$ 24,600	
Accounts Receivable	$ 65,000		
Less Allowance for Uncollectible Accounts	1,200	63,800	
Materials Inventory Control		20,400	
Work in Process Inventory Control		24,950	
Finished Goods Inventory Control		76,500	
Prepaid Insurance		3,200	
Small Tools		7,100	
Total Current Assets			$220,550
Plant and Equipment			
Machinery and Equipment	$138,500		
Less Accumulated Depreciation	64,500	$ 74,000	
Factory Building	$294,800		
Less Accumulated Depreciation	124,200	170,600	
Total Plant and Equipment			244,600
Total Assets			$465,150

Liabilities

Current Liabilities			
Accounts Payable	$ 26,100		
Wages and Salaries Payable	2,421		
Withholding Taxes Payable	1,139		
Federal Income Taxes Payable	31,220		
Interest Payable	1,250		
Total Current Liabilities		$ 62,130	
Long-Term Debt			
Notes Payable		100,000	
Total Liabilities			$162,130

Stockholders' Equity

Capital Stock		$250,000	
Retained Earnings, January 1, 19xx	$ 21,800		
Net Income for 19xx	31,220		
Retained Earnings, December 31, 19xx		53,020	
Total Stockholders' Equity			303,020
Total Liabilities and Stockholders' Equity			$465,150

Working Papers

1-3 Journal entries prepared

		General Journal			
Date		Description	Post. Ref.	Debit	Credit

Computations:

4 *Journal entry prepared*

		General Journal	Post. Ref.	Debit	Credit
Date		Description			

Computation:

Problem 15A-4
Partnership Liquidation

1-5 Journal entries prepared

Date	Description	Post. Ref.	Debit	Credit

	General Journal				
Date	Description	Post. Ref.	Debit	Credit	
19x1					

Calculation:	Stein	Caffoe	Loss Distributed

		General Journal			
Date		Description	Post. Ref.	Debit	Credit
19x2					
Jan.	1				

Calculation:		

General Journal

Date	Description	Post. Ref.	Debit	Credit
19x2				
Dec. 31				

Calculation:	Stein	Caffoe	Austin	Income Distributed

		General Journal			
Date		Description	Post. Ref.	Debit	Credit
19x3					

Stein, Caffoe, and Austin Partnership
Statement of Liquidation
January 1, 19x3

Explanation	Cash	Accounts Receivable	Land	Building (Net)	Office Equipment (Net)	Accounts Payable	Mortgage Payable	Stein, Capital	Caffoe, Capital	Austin, Capital	Gain or (Loss) from Realization
Balance 1/1/x3	$122,000	$76,000	$18,000	$140,000	$54,000	$54,000	$102,000	$84,480	$105,520	$64,000	0

1 *Journal entries prepared*

		General Journal			
Date		Description	Post. Ref.	Debit	Credit

2 *Stockholders' equity section prepared*

Fast Rail Company		
Stockholders' Equity		
July 31, 19xx		

Problem 16A-3
Preferred and Common Stock Dividends

1 Dividends computed for common and cumulative preferred stock

	Preferred Stock Dividends		Common Stock Dividends		Total Dividends Allocated
	Amount	Per Share	Amount	Per Share	

2 Dividends computed for common and noncumulative, fully participating preferred stock

	Preferred Stock Dividends		Common Stock Dividends		Total Dividends Allocated
	Amount	Per Share	Amount	Per Share	

1 *Preferred stock book value per share*

2 *Common stock book value per share*

45

1 Taxable income determined

2 Tax liability determined

Yates Corporation		
Summary of Federal Income Tax Data		
For the Tax Year		

1 Journal entries prepared

	General Journal			
Date	Description	Post. Ref.	Debit	Credit

2· Stockholders' equity section of balance sheet prepared

Mota Clothing Company		
Stockholders' Equity		
September 30, 19x2		

Problem 17A-5
Corporate Income Statement

Jorgenson Shoe Company					
Income Statement					
For the Year Ended December 31, 19xx					

1 *Journal entries prepared*

Date	Description	Post. Ref.	Debit	Credit

1 (continued)

		General Journal	Post. Ref.	Debit	Credit
Date		Description			

1 (continued)

		General Journal			
Date		Description	Post. Ref.	Debit	Credit

2 Statement of retained earnings prepared

Galloway Company		
Statement of Retained Earnings		
For the Year Ended December 31, 19xx		

3 *Stockholders' equity section prepared*

Galloway Company
Stockholder's Equity
December 31, 19xx

Problem 18A-1
Bond Transactions

1 *Journal entries prepared for bonds issued at face value*

2 *Journal entries prepared for bonds issued at more than face value*

		General Journal	Post. Ref.	Debit	Credit
Date		Description			

2 (continued)

3 Journal entries prepared for bonds issued at less than face value

		General Journal			
Date		Description	Post. Ref.	Debit	Credit

1 Mortgage payment schedule prepared

Payment Date	Unpaid Balance at Beginning of Period	Monthly Payment	Interest for One Month at 1% on Unpaid Balance	Reduction in Debt	Unpaid Balance at End of Period

2 *Journal entries prepared*

		General Journal			
Date		Description	Post. Ref.	Debit	Credit

2 (continued)

		General Journal			
Date		Description	Post. Ref.	Debit	Credit

Problem 18A-4
Bond Retirements and Conversions

1 Interest and amortization table prepared

Semiannual Interest Payment	Carrying Value at Beginning of Period	Semiannual Interest Expense at 5.5% to Be Recorded*	Semiannual Interest to Be Paid to Bondholders	Amortization of Premium	Unamortized Bond Premium at End of Period	Carrying Value at End of Period
0						
1						
2						
3						
4						
5						
6						
7						
8						
9						
10						

*Rounded to nearest dollar.

2 Journal entries prepared

	General Journal			
Date	Description	Post. Ref.	Debit	Credit

2 (continued)

		General Journal			
Date		Description	Post. Ref.	Debit	Credit

Problem 19A-1
Effect of Transactions on Working Capital

Transaction	Increase	Decrease	No Effect
a. Recorded net income.			
b. Declared cash dividend.			
c. Issued stock for cash.			
d. Retired long-term debt by issuing stock.			
e. Paid accounts payable.			
f. Purchased inventory on credit.			
g. Purchased a one-year insurance policy.			
h. Purchased a long-term investment for cash.			
i. Sold marketable securities (at cost).			
j. Sold a machine for its book value (no gain or loss).			
k. Retired fully depreciated equipment.			

1 Work sheet prepared

	Winslow Company				
	Statement of Changes in Financial Position Work Sheet				
	For the Year Ended June 30, 19x2				
Description	Account Balances, June 30, 19x1	Analysis of Transactions Debit	Credit		Account Balances, June 30, 19x2

2 *Statement of changes in financial position prepared*

Winslow Company		
Statement of Changes in Financial Position		
For the Year Ended June 30, 19x2		

Problem 19A-4
Statement of Changes in Financial Position

1 *Work sheet prepared*

	Montoya Corporation			
	Statement of Changes in Financial Position Work Sheet			
	For the Month Ended July 31, 19x1			
Description	Account Balances, June 30, 19x1	Analysis of Transactions for July		Account Balances, July 31, 19x1
		Debit	Credit	

2 Statement of changes in financial position prepared

Montoya Corporation
Statement of Changes in Financial Position
For the Month Ended July 31, 19x1

Problem 19A-6
Cash Flow Statement

1 *Cash flow from operations computed*

2 *Cash flow statement prepared*

Sharpe Corporation		
Cash Flow Statement		
For the Year Ended June 30, 19x2		

Problem 20A-1
Long-Term Investments—Equity Method

1 *Journal entries prepared*.

		General Journal			
Date		Description	Post. Ref.	Debit	Credit

2 Ledger account prepared

	General Ledger						
Investment in Bottom Line Corporation							
		Post.				Balance	
Date	Item	Ref.	Debit	Credit	Debit	Credit	

Problem 20A-2
Long-Term Investment Transactions

		General Journal			
Date		Description	Post. Ref.	Debit	Credit

	General Journal			
Date	Description	Post. Ref.	Debit	Credit

Metz and Babbitt Corporations

Work Sheet for Consolidated Balance Sheet

December 31, 19xx

Accounts	Metz Corp. Balance Sheet	Babbitt Corp. Balance Sheet	Eliminations Debit	Eliminations Credit	Consolidated Balance Sheet

Problem 20A-4
Preparation of Consolidated Income Statement

Butcher and Staufel Corporations
Work Sheet for Consolidated Income Statement
For the Year Ended December 31, 19x2

Accounts	Butcher Corp. Income Statement	Staufel Corp. Income Statement	Eliminations Debit	Eliminations Credit	Consolidated Income Statement

Phelps and McGuire Corporations

Work Sheet for Consolidated Balance Sheet

As of Acquisition Date

Accounts	Phelps Corp. Balance Sheet	McGuire Corp. Balance Sheet	Eliminations Debit	Eliminations Credit	Consolidated Balance Sheet

Problem 20A-6
Bond Investment Transactions

		General Journal			
Date		Description	Post. Ref.	Debit	Credit

	General Journal			
Date	Description	Post. Ref.	Debit	Credit

1 Balance sheet converted: (a) self-contained subsidiary (Type I) (b) subsidiary as an integral part of States
  Corporation's operation (Type II)

	Canadian Corporation		
	Balance Sheet		
	December 31, 19xx		
Balance Sheet	Canadian Dollars	Exchange Rate	U.S. Dollars

2 *Converted income statements discussed*

Name _____

Transaction	Ratio	Effect		
		Increase	Decrease	None
a. Issued common stock for cash.	Asset turnover			
b. Declared cash dividend.	Current ratio			
c. Sold treasury stock.	Return on equity			
d. Borrowed cash by issuing a note payable.	Debt to equity			
e. Paid salary expense.	Inventory turnover			
f. Purchased merchandise for cash.	Current ratio			
g. Sold equipment for cash.	Receivable turnover			
h. Sold merchandise on account.	Quick ratio			
i. Paid current portion of long-term debt.	Return on assets			
j. Gave a sales discount.	Profit margin			
k. Purchased marketable securities for cash.	Quick ratio			
l. Declared a 5% stock dividend.	Current ratio			

1 *Trend analysis prepared*

O'Brian Corporation					
Trend Analysis					
For the Years Ended December 31, 19x5–19x1					
	19x5	19x4	19x3	19x2	19x1
Sales					
Cost of Goods Sold					
Gross Margin from Sales					
Operating Expenses					
Net Income					
Accounts Receivable					
Inventory					
Current Assets					
Current Liabilities					

2 Favorable and unfavorable trends explained

114

Problem 21A-6
Preparation of Statements from Ratios and Incomplete Data

Timbore Corporation		
Income Statement: For the Year Ended September 30, 19x1		
(in thousands of dollars)		
Sales		
Cost of Goods Sold		
Gross Margin on Sales		
Operating Expenses		
Selling Expenses	8000 —	
Administrative Expenses		
Interest Expense	1000 —	
Income Tax Expense		
Total Operating Expenses		13000 —
Net Income		

Timbore Corporation		
Balance Sheet: September 31, 19x1		
(in thousands of dollars)		
Assets		
Cash	500 —	
Accounts Receivable (net)		
Inventories		
Total Current Assets		
Property, Plant, and Equipment (net)		
Total Assets		
Liabilities and Stockholders' Equity		
Current Liabilities		
Bonds Payable		
Total Liabilities		
Capital Stock, $1 Par Value	1000 —	
Paid-in Capital in Excess of Par Value	9000 —	
Retained Earnings		
Total Stockholders' Equity		
Total Liabilities and Stockholders' Equity		

Calculations:

Problem 22A-2
Direct Materials—Cost Flow

1 Characteristics of direct and indirect materials identified

a.

b.

2 Examples listed

3 *Diagram completed*

4 Amounts computed

If paid on September 8:

If paid on September 29:

Problem 22A-3
Cost of Goods Manufactured—Three Fundamental Steps

Victoria Metallurgists, Inc.									
Schedules for Cost of Goods Manufactured									
For the Quarter Ended March 31, 19xx									
1 Cost of materials used during quarter calculated									
2 Total manufacturing costs for quarter calculated									
3 Cost of goods manufactured during quarter calculated									

135

1,2 Work sheet prepared (see page 237)

3 Financial statements prepared

Rosman Metal Fabricators, Inc.		
Statement of Cost of Goods Manufactured		
For the Year Ended December 31, 19xx		

3 (continued)

Rosman Metal Fabricators, Inc.														
Income Statement														
For the Year Ended December 31, 19xx														

3 (continued)

Rosman Metal Fabricators, Inc.			
Balance Sheet			
December 31, 19xx			

4 *Closing entries prepared*

		General Journal			
Date	Description	Post. Ref.	Debit	Credit

4 (continued)

		General Journal			
Date		Description	Post. Ref.	Debit	Credit

Problem 23A-2
Job Order Cost Flow

Transaction	Materials		Inventories		
			Work in Process	Finished Goods	
1 Beginning balances, April 1, 19xx	3 1 3 6 0 —		1 5 1 1 2 —	1 7 1 2 0 —	
2 Total cost of completed orders transferred to Finished Goods Inventory during April					
3 Total cost of units sold during April computed					

Problem 23A-3
Job Order Costing—Unknown Quantity Analysis

a.	f.
b.	g.
c.	h.
d.	i.
e.	j.

	October	November
Materials:		
Beginning balance	?	?
Purchases	47090 —	50116 —
Requisitions	(48025)—	?
Ending balance	33014 —	28628 —
Work in Process:		
Finished Goods:		

Problem 23A-5
Job Order Costing—Comprehensive Journal Entry Analysis

1 Journal entries prepared

		General Journal			
Date	Description	Post. Ref.	Debit	Credit

1 (continued)

	General Journal			
Date	Description	Post. Ref.	Debit	Credit

1 (continued)

		General Journal			
Date		Description	Post. Ref.	Debit	Credit

2 Entries posted to T accounts

Materials Inventory Control	Mixing Fluid—Subsidiary

MX Powder—Subsidiary	Operating Supplies—Subsidiary

Work in Process Inventory Control	Job 20-4—Subsidiary

Job 30-5—Subsidiary	Job 50-6—Subsidiary

Finished Goods Inventory Control	Product 20—Subsidiary

2 (continued)

Product 30—Subsidiary

Product 50—Subsidiary

Cost of Goods Sold

Factory Overhead Control

Factory Overhead Applied

Factory Payroll

Operating Supplies—Subsidiary (O/H)

Factory Rent—Subsidiary (O/H)

Heat, Light & Power—Subsidiary (O/H)

Repairs and Maintenance—Subsidiary (O/H)

Outside Contractual Services—
Subsidiary (O/H)

Indirect Labor—Subsidiary (O/H)

Factory Property Taxes—Subsidiary (O/H)

Depreciation Expense,
Machinery—Subsidiary (O/H)

3 Accuracy of control account balances checked

Materials Inventory Control:

Work in Process Inventory Control:

Finished Goods Inventory Control:

1 Schedules prepared

a. Schedule of Equivalent Production

The California Candy Company, Blending Department			
Process Cost Analysis			
For the Month Ended June 30, 19xx			
Units—Stage of Completion	Units to Be Accounted For	Equivalent Units	
		Materials Costs	Conversion Costs

b. Unit Cost Analysis Schedule

Total Cost Analysis	Costs from Beginning Inventory	Costs from Current Period	Total Costs to Be Accounted For

Computation of Equivalent Unit Cost	Total Costs to Be Accounted For	Equivalent Units	Cost per Equivalent Unit

1 (continued)

c. Cost Summary Schedule

	Cost of Goods Transferred to the Forming and Packing Department	Cost of Ending Work in Process Inventory

Computational check:		

2 Journal entry prepared

	General Journal			
Date	Description	Post. Ref.	Debit	Credit

1 Schedules prepared

a. Schedule of Equivalent Production

	Bess Wafer Company		
	Process Cost Analysis		
	For the Month Ended March 31, 19xx		
	Units to Be Accounted For	Equivalent Units	
Units—Stage of Completion		Materials Costs	Conversion Costs
Beginning Inv	56000		

b. Unit Cost Analysis Schedule

Total Cost Analysis	Costs from Beginning Inventory	Costs from Current Period	Total Costs to Be Accounted For

Computation of Equivalent Unit Cost	Total Costs to Be Accounted For	Equivalent Units	Cost per Equivalent Unit

1 (continued)

c. Cost Summary Schedule

	Cost of Goods Transferred to Finished Goods Inventory	Cost of Ending Work in Process Inventory

Computational check:		

2 Journal entry prepared

		General Journal	Post. Ref.	Debit	Credit
Date		Description			

1 Schedules prepared

a. Schedule of Equivalent Production

Abdulwahed Bottling Company, Mixing Department			
Process Cost Analysis			
For the Month Ending August 31, 19xx			
	Units to Be Accounted For	Equivalent Units	
Units—Stage of Completion		Materials Costs	Conversion Costs

b. Unit Cost Analysis Schedule

Total Cost Analysis	Costs from Beginning Inventory	Costs from Current Period	Total Costs to Be Accounted For

Computation of Equivalent Unit Cost	Total Costs to Be Accounted For	Equivalent Units	Cost per Equivalent Unit

1 (continued)

c. Cost Summary Schedule

	Cost of Goods Transferred to Bottling Department	Cost of Ending Work in Process Inventory

Computational check:		

2 Journal entry prepared

	General Journal			
Date	Description	Post. Ref.	Debit	Credit

Problem 24A-4
Process Costing—One Process and Two Time Periods

A unit analysis will help in the solution to this problem.

	April	May

Solution begins on the next page.

1 Schedules prepared for April

a. Schedule of Equivalent Production

Diefenderfer Company				
Process Cost Analysis				
For the Month Ended April 30, 19xx				
Units—Stage of Completion	Units to Be Accounted For	Equivalent Units		
		Materials Costs	Conversion Costs	

b. Unit Cost Analysis Schedule

Total Cost Analysis	Costs from Beginning Inventory	Costs from Current Period	Total Costs to Be Accounted For

Computation of Equivalent Unit Cost	Total Costs to Be Accounted For	Equivalent Units	Cost per Equivalent Unit

1 (continued)

c. Cost Summary Schedule

	Cost of Goods Transferred to Finished Goods Inventory	Cost of Ending Work in Process Inventory

Computational check:		

2 Journal entry prepared for April

Date	Description	Post. Ref.	Debit	Credit

3 Schedules and journal entry prepared for May

a. Schedule of Equivalent Production

	Diefenderfer Company				
	Process Cost Analysis				
	For the Month Ended May 31, 19xx				
	Units to Be		Equivalent Units		
	Accounted			Conversion	
Units—Stage of Completion	For		Materials Costs	Costs	

b. Unit Cost Analysis Schedule

	Costs from	Costs from	Total Costs
	Beginning	Current	to Be
Total Cost Analysis	Inventory	Period	Accounted For

	Total Costs		Cost per
Computation of	to Be	Equivalent	Equivalent
Equivalent Unit Cost	Accounted For	Units	Unit

3 (continued)

c. Cost Summary Schedule

	Cost of Goods Transferred to Finished Goods Department					Cost of Ending Work in Process Inventory				

Computational check:										

General Journal

Date	Description	Post. Ref.	Debit	Credit

A unit analysis in the space below will help in the solution to this problem.

	Mixing Department	Cooking Department

Solution begins on the next page.

1 Schedules prepared for the Mixing Department

a. Schedule of Equivalent Production

	Units to Be Accounted For	Equivalent Units	
Cheng Foods, Inc., Mixing Department			
Process Cost Analysis			
For the Month Ending January 31, 19xx			
Units—Stage of Completion		Materials Costs	Conversion Costs

b. Unit Cost Analysis Schedule

Total Cost Analysis	Costs from Beginning Inventory	Costs from Current Period	Total Costs to Be Accounted For

Computation of Equivalent Unit Cost	Total Costs to Be Accounted For	Equivalent Units	Cost per Equivalent Unit

1 (continued)

c. Cost Summary Schedule

	Cost of Goods Transferred to Cooking Department	Cost of Ending Work in Process Inventory

Computational check:		

2 Journal entry prepared

	General Journal			
Date	Description	Post. Ref.	Debit	Credit

3 Schedules for Cooking Department and journal entry prepared

a. Schedule of Equivalent Production

Cheng Foods, Inc., Cooking Department			
Process Cost Analysis			
For the Month Ending January 31, 19xx			
Units—Stage of Completion	Units to Be Accounted For	Equivalent Units	
		Transferred-in Costs	Conversion Costs

b. Unit Cost Analysis Schedule

Total Cost Analysis	Costs from Beginning Inventory	Costs from Current Period	Total Costs to Be Accounted For

Computation of Equivalent Unit Cost	Total Costs to Be Accounted For	Equivalent Units	Cost per Equivalent Unit

3 (continued)

c. Cost Summary Schedule

	Cost of Goods Transferred to Canning Department	Cost of Ending Work in Process Inventory

Computational check:		

General Journal				
Date	Description	Post. Ref.	Debit	Credit

1 Break-even units computed

2 Break-even dollars computed

3 Break-even units computed with higher fixed costs

4 Break-even units computed with changed selling price and costs

1 Type of Cost/Cost Objective   *Allocation Base*

1. Cost of corporate computer center/

   production departments

   Discussion:

2. Depreciation of division factory buildings/

   production departments

   Discussion:

3. Tool and die making cost (service department)/

   production departments

   Discussion:

1 (continued)   *Allocation Base*

4. Material storage costs/

   products

   Discussion:

5. Repairs and maintenance department costs/

   production departments

   Discussion:

2 Disadvantage and advantage

1a Break-even point in units

1b Target units computed

2 Units computed for higher profit and higher cost

3 Selling price determined

4 Increased amount for advertising determined

1 Schedule prepared

Total hours of usage =			
Cost per hour of usage =			
Department	Usage Hours	Cost per Hour of Usage	Total Cost Allocation

2 *Cost allocation bases identified and compared*

1 Joint costs computed by physical volume method

Product	Liters Produced	Allocation Ratio	Total Joint Costs	Joint Cost Allocation
Totals				

2 Joint costs computed by relative sales value approach

Product	Liters Produced	Unit Selling Price	Relative Sales Value at Split-off	Allocation Ratio*	Total Joint Costs	Joint Cost Allocation
Totals						

*Rounded to two decimal places.

3 *Two methods compared*

	Extra-Rich Blend		Quality Blend		Regular Blend	
	Physical Volume Method	Relative Sales Value Method	Physical Volume Method	Relative Sales Value Method	Physical Volume Method	Relative Sales Value Method
Sales						
Cost of Sales						
Gross Margin						
Gross Margin as Percentage of Sales						

4 *Profit computed for Extra-Rich blend*

189

1 General and administrative expense budget prepared

	19x7 Expense	19x8 Adjustment	19x8 Expense
Bandy Metal Products, Inc.			
General and Administrative Expense Budget			
19x8			
Expense Category			

2 Computer service charge distribution schedule—19x8

3 General and administrative expense allocation

1 Monthly cost information prepared

October

  Direct materials:

  Direct labor:

  Factory overhead:

193

1 (continued)

November

  Direct materials:

  Direct labor:

  Factory overhead:

1 (continued)

December

   Direct materials:

   Direct labor:

   Factory overhead:

2 *Quarterly budget prepared*

	October	November	December	Quarter Totals
Hedlund Enterprises, Inc.				
Production Cost Budget				
For the Quarter Ending December 31, 19xx				

1 19x5 budget prepared

Galley Spectaculars, Inc.												
Operating Budget/Projected Income Statement												
For the Year Ending December 31, 19x5												

2 Trend of Operations

Problem 26A-4
Cash Budget Preparation

	Mount Hawk Ski Resort, Inc.				
	Cash Budget				
	For the Year Ending December 31, 19x6				
Item	January	February	March	April– December	Total

Problem 26A-4 (continued)

Item	January	February	March	April–December	Total

Mount Hawk Ski Resort, Inc.
Cash Budget
For the Year Ending December 31, 19x6

Problem 26A-5
Master Budget Preparation

1 Forecasted monthly income statement prepared

| | | Personnel | Firm Operating | General and Administrative | |
| Month | | Cost | Overhead | Expenses | Net |
(% of Fees)	Fees	(50%)	(5% + $5,400)*	(6% + $7,000)**	Income

Abel, Adams, and Sacks, Certified Public Accountants
Forecasted Monthly Income Statement
For the Year Ending December 31, 19x8

*Includes $3,000 of depreciation

**Includes $4,000 of depreciation

2 Quarterly cash budget prepared

Abel, Adams, and Sacks, Certified Public Accountants			
Quarterly Cash Budget			
For the Year Ending December 31, 19x8			
	January–March	April–June	July–September	October–December

3 Forecasted balance sheet prepared

Abel, Adams, and Sacks, Certified Public Accountants		
Projected Balance Sheet		
As of December 31, 19x8		

1 Standard direct labor cost per unit computed

2 Direct labor costs determined for increased production

3 Direct labor costs determined for unskilled labor

1 Direct materials variances computed

	Liquid Plastic	Additive
Actual cost:		
Standard cost:		
Direct materials price variances:		
Direct materials quantity variances:		
Proof:		

2 Direct labor variances computed

	Molding	Trimming	Packing
Actual cost:			
Standard cost:			
Direct labor rate variances:			
Direct labor efficiency variances:			
Proof:			

1 Total standard direct materials cost computed

2 Standard unit cost for 19x6 computed

3 Journal entries prepared

		General Journal			
Date		Description	Post. Ref.	Debit	Credit

Direct materials variances:

1. Direct materials price variance computed

2. Direct materials quantity variance computed

Proof:

Direct labor variances:

3. Direct labor rate variance computed

4. Direct labor efficiency variance computed

Proof:

Factory overhead variances:

5. Controllable overhead variance computed

6. Overhead volume variance computed

Proof:

1 *Standard cost of one gross*

2 *Journal entries prepared*

	General Journal				
Date	Description	Post. Ref.	Debit	Credit	

2 (continued)

		General Journal			
Date		Description	Post. Ref.	Debit	Credit

2 (continued)

		General Journal	Post. Ref.	Debit	Credit
Date		Description			

2 (continued)

Analysis of direct materials purchases

Analysis of direct materials requisitions

Analysis of direct labor rate variances

Analysis of direct labor efficiency variances

3 Analysis of factory overhead accounts and variances

4 *Entry to dispose of factory overhead accounts and record overhead variances*

5 *Variance accounts closed to Cost of Goods Sold*

		General Journal			
Date		Description	Post. Ref.	Debit	Credit

1 Unit costs computed

Barton Corporation	Variable Costing	Absorption Costing
Unit Costs and Ending Inventory Values		
For the Year Ending December 31, 19x9		

2 Income statements prepared

Barton Corporation		
Income Statements		
For the Year Ending December 31, 19x9		
a. Contribution format based on variable costing data		
b. Conventional format based on absorption costing data		
Proof:		

Name

1 Decision on purchase of machine, using a 14 percent desired rate of return

2 Decision on purchase of machine, using a 16 percent desired rate of return

223

3 Decision on purchase of machine using an 8 percent after-tax desired rate of return

1 Machine hours to produce one unit of each product computed

Product	Total Machine Hours	÷	Units Produced	=	Hours per Unit

2 Profitability of each product determined

Madison Machine Tool, Inc.

Sales Mix Analysis

Contribution Reporting Format

	Products			
	14E	27M	19S	30T

3 *Decisions on product lines made*

1 *Incremental analysis prepared*

	Azusa Refrigerator Company			
	Incremental Decision Analysis			
	Current Year—Annual Usage			
		Make	Difference in Favor of Make	Buy

2 *Unit costs computed*

1 *Decision analysis prepared*

2 *Lowest price determined*

1 Analysis prepared

a. Pretax accounting rate of return method

	Increase in Net Income		
	Net Cash Inflow	Depreciation	Net Income

1 (continued)

b. Payback period method

1 (continued)

c. Present value method (minimum desired return = 12%)

Year	Net Cash Inflows	×	Present Value Multipliers (12%) from Table B-3	=	Present Value

2 After-tax analysis

a. Accounting rate of return method

Year	Net Cash Inflow	Depreciation	Income Before Taxes	Taxes	After-Tax Income

2 (continued)

b. Payback period method

2 (continued)

c. Present value method (minimum desired return = 8%)

Year	Net After-Tax Cash Inflows	×	Present Value Multipliers (8%) from Table B-3	=	Present Value